EDGE
BOOKS

MAGIC TRICKS

CAPSTONE PRESS PRESENTS

AMAZING

MAGIC

TRICKS

BEGINNER

LEVEL

by NORM BARNHART

Capstone
press®

Mankato, Minnesota

Edge Books are published by Capstone Press,
151 Good Counsel Drive, P.O. Box 669, Mankato, Minnesota 56002.
www.capstonepress.com

Library of Congress Cataloging-in-Publication Data
Barnhart, Norm.
    Amazing magic tricks: beginner level / by Norm Barnhart.
    p. cm. — (Edge books. Magic Tricks.)
    Includes bibliographical references and index.
    Summary: "Step-by-step instructions and clear photos describe how to
perform magic tricks at the beginner level" — Provided by publisher.
    ISBN-13: 978-1-4296-1942-4 (hardcover)
    ISBN-10: 1-4296-1942-2 (hardcover)
    1. Magic tricks — Juvenile literature. 1. Title. II. Series.
GV1548.B3533 2009
793.8 — dc22   2008002572

Editorial Credits
Aaron Sautter, editor; Bob Lentz, designer/illustrator; Marcy Morin, scheduler

Photo Credits
Capstone Press/Karon Dubke, cover, objects, magic steps
Shutterstock/Chen Ping Hung; javarman; Marilyn Volan;
    Tatiana53; Tischenko Irina, backgrounds

Capstone Press thanks Anthony Wacholtz of Compass Point Books and
Hilary Wacholz of Picture Window Books for their help in producing this book.

1 2 3 4 5 6 13 12 11 10 09 08

TABLE OF CONTENTS

BOOK 1

AMAZING MAGIC!

You don't need to be a master magician to perform magic. With this book, you'll learn simple, fun tricks that will amaze your friends. You can make objects magically appear or disappear right before their eyes! It's easy when you know the secret. Pick up your magic wand and get ready to learn some amazing magic!

THE KEYS TO MAGIC

→ Practice, practice, practice! If you want your tricks to work right, you need to practice until you can do them quickly and smoothly. Try standing in front of a mirror while practicing. Then you can see what the tricks will look like to your audience.

→ Keep it secret! Magicians never share their secrets. If you reveal the secrets of a trick, people won't be very impressed. It also ruins the trick for other magicians who want to do it in the future.

→ Be entertaining! Try telling the audience some jokes or stories that relate to your tricks while performing them. Keep the audience entertained, and they won't notice how the tricks are done. It will also keep them coming back for more.

BEFORE YOU BEGIN

Most magicians hide their props in a magic box. A magic box will help you keep your tricks organized and your special props hidden from the audience. You can make your own magic box. Find a cardboard box and decorate it with some colorful stars, or cover it with dark cloth so it looks mysterious.

A magic wand is one of a magician's most useful tools. Wands help direct people's attention to what you want them to see. You can make a wand out of a wooden dowel painted black and white. Or roll up a piece of black construction paper and tape the ends. You can add sparkles and stars if you wish. Be creative and have fun!

A MAGIC SECRET - PALMING

Magicians often use a method called palming to make things appear to vanish out of thin air. To do it, they secretly hide an object in the palm of their hand. Try practicing palming in front of a mirror so your hand looks natural. Once you learn to palm objects, you'll be able to amaze your friends!

THE MAGICAL SAILOR'S KNOT

Magicians need fast hands. In this trick, you'll make a knot instantly appear on a rope. Your friends will be amazed at your incredible hand speed!

WHAT YOU NEED:

→ A piece of rope about 2 feet (0.6 meters) long

PREPARATION:

1. Tie a large knot in one end of the rope as shown.

PERFORMANCE:

2. First, show the audience the rope. Hold it with the knot secretly hidden in your hand as shown.

Hidden knot

3. Now hold the other end of the rope between your thumb and first finger as shown. Be sure to keep the knot hidden. Tell the audience that your hands are faster than the eye, and that you can make a knot appear out of thin air.

4. With your free hand, pretend to grab an invisible knot out of the air. Then toss it at the rope.

As you toss the invisible knot, let go of the untied end. Say, "Oops, I missed. I'll try again."

5. Hold the untied end up like before. Pretend to throw the invisible knot again and drop the untied end. Say, "Wow, I missed again." Act a bit disappointed and then try a third time.

The third time it will work. This time let go of the end with the knot. The knot magically appears on the rope!

magic tip: By failing at first, the audience will be more amazed when you make the knot seem to magically appear.

TRICKY TREATS

Everybody loves candy. Wouldn't it be great if you could make candy appear out of nowhere? You can do just that with this quick and easy hanky trick.

WHAT YOU NEED:

- → A colorful handkerchief
- → A piece of wrapped candy

PREPARATION:

1. Hold the candy between your thumb and fingers as shown. It's best to use wrapped candy so your hand doesn't get sticky.

2. Next, hold the hanky in the fingers of the same hand so the candy is hidden. The audience will think you're only holding the hanky.

3. Wave the hanky in the air and act as if it's empty. Nobody should suspect that you're hiding the candy in that hand. Then place the hanky over the palm of your empty hand as shown.

4. Next, drag the hanky across your open hand. Show the audience that your hand is empty. This step helps people believe there is nothing there.

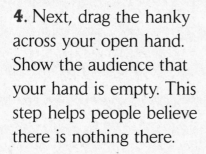

5. Now pull the hanky across your hand again. This time, drop the candy into your open hand. The candy magically appears! Give the candy to someone in the audience to enjoy during the show.

FIND THE MAGIC RABBIT

Lots of magicians like pulling rabbits out of their hats. But there's more than one way to find a magic rabbit. In this trick, a magical paper bunny is the star of the show!

WHAT YOU NEED:

→ A marker or crayon
→ A colorful handkerchief
→ A sheet of paper

PREPARATION:

1. Draw a carrot, a bunny, and a hat on the paper as shown. Make sure the bunny is in the middle section. Leave plenty of space between each picture.

PERFORMANCE:

2. First, show the audience the paper with the three pictures. Then fold the paper between the pictures and tear it into three pieces along the folds.

3. Next, turn the pictures upside down. Ask a volunteer to mix the pictures up and cover them with the hanky while your back is turned.

4. When the volunteer is finished, turn back to the table. With a mysterious look on your face say, "I can find the bunny without looking under the hanky." Then reach under the hanky to get the rabbit.

5. Now pull out the picture of the rabbit and take a bow! The secret to this trick is easy. When you reach under the hanky, simply feel the sides of each piece of paper. Since the rabbit is drawn on the center piece, it is the only paper with two torn sides. It's a simple trick that will keep your friends guessing how it's done!

Torn sides

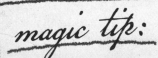

magic tip: Try this trick with some different drawings. You could draw the faces of two boys and a girl, or two dogs and a cat.

JACK, THE INCREDIBLE CARD

That Jack of Diamonds is one strong card. This super stunt will amaze your friends. They'll watch in wonder as Jack balances a cup on his top edge!

WHAT YOU NEED:

- → One Jack of Diamonds card
- → One other card
- → A foam cup
- → Tape
- → Scissors

PREPARATION:

1. First, cut the extra card in half lengthwise as shown.

2. Next, tape one half of the cut card to the back of the Jack of Diamonds as shown. This creates a secret flap. When the flap is down, the back of the Jack should look like a normal card.

3. Hold up the cup and the Jack card. Show the audience both sides of the card and say, "Jack looks like a normal card, but he's really strong. He can do an amazing balancing act."

4. Now place the cup on the edge of the card. Secretly bring out the flap to balance the cup as shown.

5. Finally, pull your hand away to show that the Jack card is balancing the cup. Ask the audience to give Jack a round of applause and have him take a bow!

magic tip: Always keep the back of the card toward you when the flap is out. Otherwise the secret of the trick will be revealed.

WONDERFUL APPEARING WAND

Every magician needs a magic wand. This trick will astound your audience as your magic wand appears in an impossible way.

WHAT YOU NEED:

> A magic wand
> A large box of candy
> A jacket or shirt with long sleeves
> Scissors

PREPARATION:

1. First, take the candy out of the box and save some for later. Then cut a small hole in the bottom of the box. Make sure the hole is a little larger than your magic wand.

2. Next, slide the wand up your sleeve as shown. When you're ready to do the trick, you'll simply slide the wand through the hole in the box. Put the candy you saved back in the box.

2. Close your hand around the wand and put the bottle back in your magic box.

Now grip your wrist with your other hand and slide your finger up to hold the wand as shown. Don't let your friends see your finger or the trick will be ruined!

3. Next, slowly open your hand to show that the wand is stuck in place. Say, "This invisible glue is some really sticky stuff!"

4. When you want the glue to disappear, just ask a friend to snap his or her fingers. At that moment, let the wand go by moving your finger. The wand is no longer stuck to your hand!

AMAZING APPEARING BALL

"Where did that ball come from?" That's what your friends will say when you make this ball magically appear from an empty cup!

WHAT YOU NEED:

- A ping-pong ball
- A foam cup
- A magic wand

PREPARATION:

1. First, poke a hole in the foam cup so your finger can slip into it.

Now place the ball in the cup and use your third finger to hold it in place as shown.

magic fact: Add some fun to this trick by drawing a face on the ball and giving it a fun name. Pretend that it likes to play hide-and-seek!

2. First tip over the cup to show that it's empty. Then tell the audience, "Things aren't always how they appear. This cup might look empty, but it's not." Be sure not to let anyone see the ball or your finger inside the cup!

3. Now hold the cup up high and wave your magic wand over it. While you do this, you can say a few made-up magic words, if you want.

4. Finally, tip over the cup and let the ball fall into your open hand. The ball magically appears!

Show the audience the ball and toss it to someone. While they're looking at it, drop the special cup into your magic box. Nobody will ever know the secret!

THE FANTASTIC FLOWER

Flowers grow quickly in the spring. But with this trick, you can make a flower appear instantly with special magic seeds. Your friends will be really impressed!

WHAT YOU NEED:

+ A small flower pot
+ A fake flower
+ An empty seed packet
+ A magic wand

PREPARATION:

1. Place the flower in the flower pot. Then put the pot in your magic box.

PERFORMANCE:

2. When you're ready to do this trick, hide the flower by holding it against the side of the pot as shown.

Hidden flower

3. Hold up the pot so the audience can see that it's empty. Be sure to keep the flower hidden under your hand.

4. Tell the audience about your magic flower seeds. Say, "These are the world's fastest growing flowers." Pretend to sprinkle some invisible seeds from the seed packet into the flower pot.

Next, wave your magic wand over the pot and say a few magic words.

5. Now reach in and pull out the pretty flower that has magically grown inside! You can give the flower to your mom or a friend as a gift.

THE MYSTERIOUS CAR TRICK

You can use the power of your mind to find a shiny, cool car hidden in a paper bag. Your incredible mental powers will baffle people with this trick!

WHAT YOU NEED:

+ Three small paper bags
+ One shiny cool toy car
+ Two dull toy cars
+ A pencil

PREPARATION:

1. Place a small, secret pencil mark in the lower right corner of one bag as shown. Don't make the mark too dark or someone might see it and learn how this trick works.

PERFORMANCE:

2. First, show the three cars to the audience. Place the shiny cool car in the marked bag. Place the dull cars in the other bags. Then fold over the tops of all three bags. Keep the secret mark facing you so nobody sees it.

Secret mark

3. Tell the audience about your amazing mental powers. Say, "I can use my mind to find the cool car, even if the bags are mixed up." Then turn around and ask a volunteer from the audience to mix up the bags.

4. Now turn back to the table and pretend to use your mind powers to find the cool car. Hold up each bag and look at it closely. Pretend to concentrate hard on what's inside. While doing this, you will really be looking for the bag with the secret mark.

5. When you find the marked bag say, "This is it! I've found the cool car." Reach in and pull out the cool car. Take a bow as the audience applauds your amazing mental powers!

magic tip: Try acting like you don't know which bag is correct at first. The audience will be even more amazed when you find the cool car!

ZARCON, THE INVISIBLE HERO

The alien hero Zarcon has worked hard to bring criminals to justice. Now it's time for him to go home. With a wave of your magic wand, he disappears and travels back to his own planet.

WHAT YOU NEED:

→ A colorful handkerchief
→ A small action figure
→ A secret helper
→ A magic wand

PERFORMANCE:

1. Show Zarcon to the audience and tell them he wants to return to his home planet. Tell them that you're going to help him with a bit of magic. When you're ready for the trick, hold the toy in your hand as shown.

2. Next, place the hanky over your hand to hide Zarcon as shown.

3. Now ask two volunteers to feel under the hanky to make sure Zarcon hasn't disappeared yet.

4. The second person will really be your secret helper. Your helper will secretly take Zarcon from your hand as shown, and then hide the toy in his or her pocket. Ask your secret helper, "Is Zarcon still there?" He or she should say, "Yes."

5. After your helper takes Zarcon, wave your magic wand over the hanky. Finally, remove the hanky and show the audience that Zarcon has disappeared!

magic tip: Be sure to practice this trick with your helper ahead of time. Make it look smooth and natural and the audience won't suspect a thing.

FAST RABBIT AND THE ACE

People love card tricks. They love to watch cards magically switch locations or change colors. In this trick, your magic rabbit loves the Ace of Diamonds so much he can't resist stealing it!

WHAT YOU NEED:

> A deck of cards
> A small stuffed bunny
> A table

PREPARATION:

1. First, separate the four aces from the deck of cards. Place the Ace of Diamonds on top of the deck of cards. Then set the other three aces on top of the Ace of Diamonds.

magic tip: If you don't have a bunny, you can use any other small stuffed toy for this trick.

2. Introduce your stuffed bunny to the audience. Tell them he really loves the Ace of Diamonds. Say that he sometimes steals it so fast that you can't even see him move!

Take the three aces from the top of the deck and set them aside. Be sure to leave the Ace of Diamonds on top of the deck. Then place the bunny on top of the deck.

3. Arrange the three aces with the Ace of Hearts in the middle as shown. Hold the cards close together so the Ace of Hearts looks like the Ace of Diamonds as shown in the second picture above. Then ask a volunteer to help with this trick. Show the volunteer the aces. Ask if he or she sees the Ace of Diamonds. The volunteer should say, "Yes."

TURN PAGE FOR MORE!

4. Next, lay the aces one by one face down on the table. Make sure the volunteer doesn't see the front of the cards. Ask the volunteer to guess which card is the Ace of Diamonds. He or she will probably pick the middle card.

5. Flip the card over to show that it is really the Ace of Hearts. Your volunteer will probably be surprised! Ask the volunteer to try picking a different card.

6. Flip over the next chosen card. It won't be the Ace of Diamonds either. Do this again with the third card so all three aces are face up.

7. It's time to show where the Ace of Diamonds went. Say, "Look at that — the Ace of Diamonds is gone! I bet my magic bunny ran over and stole it so fast that we couldn't see it."

Lift the bunny off the deck of cards. Pick up the top card and show that he's been sitting on the Ace of Diamonds! Thank your volunteer and have the bunny take a bow.

GLOSSARY

astound (uh-STOUND) — to amaze or astonish

audience (AW-dee-uhns) — people who watch or listen to a play, movie, or show

concentrate (KAHN-suhn-trayt) — to focus your thoughts and attention on something

dowel (DOUL) — a round wooden rod

mental power (MEN-tuhl POW-ur) — the ability to do something with the mind, such as finding hidden objects or reading others' thoughts

palming (PALM-ing) — to hide something in the palm of your hand

prop (PROP) — an item used by an actor or performer during a show

volunteer (vol-uhn-TIHR) — someone who offers to help perform a task during a show

READ MORE

Ho, Oliver. *Young Magician: Magic Tricks.*
New York: Sterling, 2003.

Longe, Bob. *Easy Hand Tricks.* New York:
Sterling, 2003.

Zenon, Paul. *Simple Sleight-of-Hand: Card and
Coin Tricks for the Beginning Magician.* Amazing
Magic. New York: Rosen, 2008.

INTERNET SITES

FactHound offers a safe, fun way to find Internet
sites related to this book. All of the sites on
FactHound have been researched by our staff.

Here's how:
1. Visit *www.facthound.com*
2. Choose your grade level.
3. Type in this book ID **1429619422** for age-appropriate
   sites. You may also browse subjects by clicking on letters,
   or by clicking on pictures and words.
4. Click on the **Fetch It** button.

FactHound will fetch the best sites for you!

About the author

Norm Barnhart is a professional comic magician who has entertained audiences for more than 28 years. In 2007, Norm was named America's Funniest Magician by the Family Entertainers Workshop. Norm's travels have taken him across the United States and to five other countries. Norm also loves getting kids excited about reading. Norm says, "I love bringing smiles to people's faces with magic. After reading this book, kids will love doing magic too."